GENTES GENTES

I Longed For You

Contents

1

Mother's Sacrifice

In the late 1980s, amidst the vibrant landscapes of Dominica, Derrick came into the world, cradled in the arms of his single mother, Cynthia Duncan. Her heart overflowed with joy as she welcomed her one and only child, a son, into the embrace of life. At the tender age of 25, the warmth of maternal love enveloped her, fulfilling a longing she had carried for years.

But joy often dances hand in hand with sorrow, and for Cynthia, this truth was painfully evident. Financial struggles weighed heavily on her shoulders, exacerbated by the absence of support from Derrick 's father, James Norbert. Despite her fierce desire to be with her son every moment, the harsh realities of life forced her to make a heart-wrenching decision.

With reluctance etched into every fibre of her being, Cynthia made the agonizing choice to seek employment from a neighbouring island, leaving behind her beloved son, just a year old, in the care of her parents. The pain of separation cut deep, tearing at the fragile bonds of mother and child. As she embarked on her journey, her heart remained tethered to her son, aching with each step taken away from him.

For Derrick, the absence of his mother cast a shadow over his early years, a void he sought to fill with the love and support of his grandparents, aunts, and uncles. In the absence of his father, who remained miles away, the extended family became his pillars of strength, nurturing him with unwavering devotion.

In the embrace of his grandmother, he found solace, his tiny arms reaching out for the comfort he craved, unaware of the weight of his mother's absence. In the innocence of childhood, he bestowed upon his grandmother the title of "mummy," a testament to the love that bound them together.

Navigating the intricate maze of his formative years, the echoes of his mother's sacrifice reverberated through his life. Each milestone reached, each hurdle overcome, stood as a testament to her enduring love and unwavering determination. Though separated by miles, the bond between mother and son remained unbroken, a thread weaving through the fabric of their shared existence.

In the absence of his father, he found refuge in the arms of his family, their love serving as a signal of optimism amidst the stormy seas of life. Through their guidance and support, he learned the true meaning of resilience, forging ahead despite the challenges that lay before him.

As the years passed, his journey unfolded, shaped by the love, loss, and resilience that defined his early years. Though the road ahead may be fraught with obstacles, he walked it with courage, his heart filled with the enduring love of a mother's sacrifice. And in the depths of his soul, he carried the indelible imprint of her unwavering love, a guiding light illuminating his path.

In the textile of life, Derrick 's story was but a single thread, woven with the threads of countless others, each contributing to the rich fabric of human experience. And as he embarked on the journey that lay before him, he carried with him the lessons learned, the memories cherished, and the love that bound him to those who had shaped his destiny.

2

A Son's Pursuit of Self-Discovery

Derrick 's upbringing was marked by the conspicuous absence of his father. Sparse visits during his childhood and eventual disappearance left him yearning to remember his father's face, yet he could only rely on the murmurs of family and friends remarking on his striking resemblance to the man he barely knew.

Witnessing his cousins disciplined with belts by their father, he couldn't help but ponder if this was the norm for paternal behaviour. At times, he found relief in the absence of his father, fearing he might have faced similar disciplinary measures. Despite this uncertainty, he was a disciplined child, dedicated to his studies, earning praise from his aunts and grandparents.

As he transitioned from childhood to adolescence, the desire to connect with his father persisted, though tempered by acceptance of his absence. Fragmented memories flickered in his mind—the fleeting moments of paternal presence, a cup of ice cream shared, a handful of coins for snacks during rare visits parked outside in his father's car. His father's mention of his sibling Delvan and a visit from Giselle, and Emma—stirred a longing for family ties, particularly sisters, though the brief encounter failed to satisfy his yearning.

One memorable instance, his father's voice crackled through the telephone landline, prompting Derrick to withhold the endearment "daddy." When questioned, his response was simple: "I am not use to it". Even during celebrations like his First Communion, where family bonds were typically reinforced, his father made a fleeting appearance, his presence a mere formality against the backdrop of Derrick 's devout Catholic upbringing instilled by his maternal grandparents.

Despite the absence of paternal guidance, his grandparents sowed the seeds of faith within him from a tender age, nurturing his spiritual growth and providing stability in the absence of a fatherly figure. Their unwavering love and guidance shaped his character, instilling in him values that transcended the void left by his father's departure.

As he navigated the complexities of adolescence, he grappled with questions of identity and belonging. The absence of paternal influence left him searching for a sense of self, often seeking validation in the echoes of his father's fleeting presence. Yet, amidst the longing, he found solace in the bonds forged with his extended family, whose unwavering support provided a pillar of strength in his journey of self-discovery.

Through the lens of his own experiences, he came to understand that fatherhood transcended mere biological connection—it was the embodiment of love, guidance, and support, qualities he found in abundance within his familial circle. Though the absence of his father cast a shadow over his formative years, he emerged resilient, his identity forged not in the image of his absent father, but in the love and guidance of those who stood by him through life's trials and tribulations.

Within life's intricate weave, the absence of his father served as a thread of uncertainty, weaving through his journey with poignant reminders of longing and loss. Yet, amidst the void, he found strength in the bonds of family and faith, shaping him into the resilient individual he was destined to become. As he embarked on the path to adulthood, he carried with him the lessons learned from his father's absence, embracing the love and support that surrounded him, knowing that true paternal guidance transcended the limitations of mere presence.

3

A Journey of Longing and Acceptance

Derrick 's childhood was painted with hues of laughter and joy, woven into the fabric of his days spent with cousins who resided nearby. Together, they revelled in the simple pleasures of youth—playing cricket in the neighbourhood, indulging in the sweet nectar of ripe mangoes by the riverbank, and savouring the camaraderie of shared moments. These memories became treasures to him, cherished amidst the backdrop of a fragmented family dynamic.

Despite the warmth of familial bonds, he harboured a lingering void—a yearning for his mother's unwavering presence. Her sporadic visits brought fleeting moments of joy, but with each departure, his heart ached with the weight of separation. Tears were shed in silent plea, begging for her to stay a moment longer, to fill the void that her absence carved.

However, as the sands of time sifted through his fingers, his tears dried, replaced by a resigned acceptance of his mother's transient presence. The ache of longing dulled as he matured into his teenage years, understanding the constraints of her responsibilities that tethered her to distant shores. Yet, amidst the acceptance lay the seeds of detachment, Derrick struggled to bridge the emotional chasm that divided them.

Communication became a hurdle, the distance between them not only measured in miles but also in the unspoken words that hung heavy in the air. he found it difficult to reach out, the weight of their fractured relationship casting a shadow over his attempts to connect. The phone always remained silent more often than not, conversations relegated to sporadic exchanges rather than the steady flow of relative dialogue.

Despite the physical chasm that separated them, his mother remained steadfast in her commitment to provide the best life possible for her son. Her sacrifices echoed across the expanse of time and distance, a testament to her enduring love and devotion. Derrick, in turn, held onto the memories of their brief reunions, etching them into the tapestry of his childhood, each visit a beacon of warmth amidst the cool embrace of separation.

The four fleeting trips to his mother's now hometown became pillars of his childhood where moments of unbridled joy were ensconced within the embrace of his mother's love. The unfamiliar landscape of the island offered him a glimpse into a world beyond his own seeing the children's playground at McDonald's, a playground of wonder and delight which was a stark contrast to the familiar streets of Dominica.

As his mother found solace and stability of her hometown,

her presence became a constant fixture in his life, albeit from a distance. Her journey mirrored his own with each step forward being a testament to resilience and fortitude in the face of adversity. Despite the physical chasm that separated them, he found solace in the knowledge that his mother's love transcended boundaries, an invisible thread that bound them together across oceans and continents.

As he ventured into adulthood, the echoes of his childhood reverberated within him, shaping the contours of his identity. The longing for maternal presence softened into a quiet appreciation for the sacrifices made on his behalf, the moments of separation tempered by the enduring bond of love. He carried with him the lessons learned from the ebb and flow of familial ties, each thread woven with the resilience of the human spirit.

4

Awakening of Faith

Derrick 's upbringing was steeped in the traditions of faith, nurtured by the tender hands of his grandparents who sowed the seeds of devotion within his young heart. Yet, despite their efforts, he had not forged a deep connection with God, his spiritual journey fraught with uncertainty and doubt. It wasn't until the dawn of his eighteenth year, amidst the hallowed halls of a weekend retreat with his Catholic church youth group, that his soul was set ablaze with the fervour of newfound faith.

The retreat proved to be a crucible of transformation, a sacred space where his dormant spirituality was stirred from its slumber. Amidst the chorus of hymns and the solemn cadence of prayer, he felt a stirring within his soul, a whisper of divine presence that beckoned him towards enlightenment. It was a liberation of spirit, as the seeds of faith, once dormant, sprouted forth in a radiant bloom of revelation.

The defining moment of Derrick 's spiritual awakening came

in a moment of profound revelation, witnessed through the struggles of his cousin, Bernadette. As the group gathered in fervent prayer, he watched in awe as Bernadette battled with an unseen force, her lips faltering at the utterance of the name "Jesus." Confusion gripped his heart as he bore witness to this inexplicable phenomenon, his mind reeling with questions left unanswered.

Yet, amidst the tumult of uncertainty, he found solace in the collective prayers of the group, each supplication a symbol of hope amidst the darkness. And then, in a moment of divine intervention, the spirit of God descended upon Bernadette, her voice echoing with the fervor of revelation as she cried out the sacred name, "Jesus!" It was a moment of transcendent beauty, a testament to the power of faith and the boundless love of the Divine.

For Derrick, this experience marked the dawn of a new chapter in his spiritual journey—a journey illuminated by the radiant light of divine revelation. The love of Christ, once a distant concept, now pulsed within his veins, infusing his being with a profound sense of purpose and belonging. It was a seed planted deep within his soul, destined to blossom into the guiding force that would shape the course of his life.

In the aftermath of this transformative encounter, he found himself enveloped in a newfound sense of spiritual clarity. The doubts and uncertainties that once clouded his path were dispelled by the radiant glow of divine presence, guiding him towards a deeper understanding of his faith and his place within the grand weaving of creation.

He reflected on his journey marvelling at the profound ways in which faith had transformed his life. What began as a seed planted by the loving hands of his grandparents had blossomed into a radiant garden of spiritual enlightenment, nourished by the waters of divine grace and illuminated by the light of divine love.

In the crucible of spiritual awakening, he discovered the true essence of faith—not merely as a set of beliefs, but as a living, breathing force that permeated every aspect of his being. It was a journey marked by moments of revelation and redemption, each step forward a testament to the transformative power of divine love.

Derrick embraced his newfound spiritual identity. He knew that his journey was far from over. With each passing day he would continue to nurture the seeds of faith planted within his soul, allowing them to flourish and grow, illumining hope and inspiration for all who crossed his path.

5

Family Threads & A Quest for Connection

At the age of twenty, a year after bidding farewell to the halls of community college and embracing the responsibilities of employment, Derrick embarked on a journey that would reshape the contours of his identity—the quest to uncover the enigmatic fabric of his paternal lineage. Armed with curiosity and propelled by a longing to unearth family ties long shrouded in mystery, he delved into the labyrinthine depths of his father's ancestry, a journey swimming with both anticipation and trepidation.

What awaited him on this odyssey of self-discovery was a revelation of staggering proportions—a sprawling network of aunts, uncles, and eleven siblings, each bearing names as varied as the hues of the Caribbean sunset. Rose, Yasmin, Manuel, Giselle, Sheldon, Manuel, Emma, Crystal, Delvan, Nia, Ethan, and the solemn remembrance of Sixtus, whose untimely demise cast a somber shadow over the family, a casualty of political tumult.

The memories of his father, James, flickered dimly in his mind, a distant echo of paternal presence that waned with the passing years. Their paths diverged when he was a mere nine years old, leaving behind a void that echoed with the whispers of unanswered questions. Yet, in the digital age's embrace, he found a lifeline—a thread of connection that transcended temporal and spatial boundaries.

The advent of social media proved to be a signal of optimism in Derrick 's quest for reconciliation. Through the digital ether, he navigated the network of virtual connections, piecing together fragments of his father's lineage until, at last, he stood on the threshold of reunion. With trembling fingers and a heart heavy with anticipation, he reached out to his father, James, across the digital divide, each keystroke a testament to the resilience of familial bonds that withstood the test of time.

The moment of reckoning arrived with a flourish of notifications— an electronic symphony that heralded the dawn of reunion. James's response echoed through the digital expanse, a burst of joy that reverberated within Derrick 's soul. The virtual dialogue that ensued, bridged the chasm of years, stitching together the fabric of familial ties long left frayed by the passage of time.

James disclosed to his son that he would be deported from Canada due to lacking the necessary documentation to remain in the country. Nonetheless, Derrick was pleased to learn that he would soon reunite with his father.

In the wake of this revelation, he grappled with a torrent of emotions—fear, uncertainty, and a gnawing sense of inevitability. Would their paths have ever crossed if not for the serendipitous embrace of social media? Was their reunion ever going to happen if he was not about to be deported?

As he pondered the intricacies of fate, he found solace in the enduring resilience of familial ties—the unbreakable bond that transcended the constraints of geography and circumstance. Though the road ahead remained fraught with uncertainty, Derrick drew strength from the knowledge that, in the labyrinth of life's uncertainties, the guiding light of love would illuminate his path forward.

In the crucible of reunion, Derrick discovered the transformative power of connection—a testament to the indomitable spirit of the human heart, capable of bridging chasms of separation with the unyielding strength of love. As he stood on the threshold of a new chapter, He embraced the uncertainty of the journey ahead, secure in the knowledge that, no matter the obstacles they faced, the bonds of family would endure, resilient and unwavering in the face of adversity.

6

Reunion of Hearts

The long-awaited moment arrived with a blend of anticipation and apprehension as Derrick 's father, James, returned to Dominica after a decade-long absence. Eagerly, he made his way to James's home, his heart aflutter with a mixture of excitement and anxiety, yearning to finally come face-to-face with the man he had longed for throughout the years.

As he crossed the threshold into James's abode, he was enveloped in a warm embrace, though comforting, his father's touch was unfamiliar but washed over him like a gentle wave. With a smile that spoke volumes, James welcomed Derrick into his home, a silent acknowledgment of the bond that had lain dormant for far too long.

In the quiet sanctuary of James's home, father and son engaged in a conversation that spanned the breadth of years lost to time. For forty-five minutes, they shared stories and exchanged pleasantries, each word a bridge spanning the chasm of separation that had divided them for so long. It was a moment of profound significance for Derrick, finally beholding the face of the man he had forgotten, his heart swelling with a bittersweet blend of emotions.

However, amidst the reunion, a stark reality emerged—one that echoed the passage of time and the irrevocable changes it wrought. James confessed to Derrick that he would have passed his own son on the street, his features altered by the inexorable march from boyhood to manhood. The realization struck Derrick with the force of a revelation, a poignant reminder of the fleeting nature of time and the swift currents of change that carried them along.

Yet, amidst the revelations, his heart harboured a lingering question—one that weighed heavy upon his soul. Why had his father neglected to inform him of the siblings who resided in Dominica, about an hour drive away from his own doorstep? The small island's geography rendered distances insignificant, yet James's omission left Derrick struggling with a sense of betrayal and disbelief.

In response, his father offered a feeble excuse, claiming he had assumed Derrick was already aware of his siblings' existence—an assertion that rang hollow in Derrick 's ears. The gravity of his father's neglect weighed heavily upon his heart, casting a shadow over the reunion that threatened to eclipse the fragile bonds of reconciliation.

What struck Derrick most profoundly was James's cavalier attitude towards his past indiscretions, his flippant dismissal of the pain and anguish he had inflicted upon his children through his absence. There were no apologies, no regrets—only the hollow echo of a life lived in the pursuit of fleeting pleasures, heedless of the scars left in its wake.

In the aftermath of their encounter, Derrick wrestled with a torrent of conflicting emotions. While the reunion had provided closure of sorts, it also laid bare the stark reality of his father's indifference—a reality that he struggled to reconcile with the newfound knowledge of his father's face.

Yet, amidst the turmoil, Derrick found solace in the knowledge that, despite his father's shortcomings, he had finally come face-to-face with the man who had once been little more than a distant memory. In the quiet recesses of his heart, he resolved to fill the void left by James's absence with the warmth of familial love—a love that transcended the limitations of blood ties and resonated with the enduring strength of the human spirit.

As Derrick reflected on his encounter with his estranged father, he found himself embracing a newfound sense of clarity. Though James had failed to take the initiative in fostering connections between his children, Derrick vowed to forge his own path—a path illuminated by the guiding light of love and forgiveness, a path that would lead him towards healing and reconciliation, one step at a time.

7

Reunion of Siblings

Derrick embarked on the journey to connect with three of his siblings who resided miles away from him. He carried with him the weight of unspoken longing, hoping to bridge the chasm of separation that had defined his relationship with his estranged siblings, Crystal, Delvan, and Nia. Residing in Dominica, these siblings had remained a distant enigma, their presence a tantalizing whisper in the web of his existence.

On the day of their long awaited meeting, Derrick felt a sense of anticipation mingled with trepidation, as if he were piecing together the fragments of a puzzle that had long eluded him. With each step towards their home, he felt the tendrils of familiarity weave around him, binding him to the shared history that awaited him within the walls of their familial abode.

Entering their home, he was greeted not by the jubilant fanfare of reunion, but by the quiet embrace of familiarity—a recognition of shared bloodlines that transcended the confines of time and distance. It was a moment of quiet solace, as he beheld the faces of his younger siblings for the first time, their features a mirror of his own, yet imbued with the unique essence of their individuality.

The reception in the room was tinged with a sense of solemnity, a reflection perhaps of the weight of their shared history and the complexities of familial bonds forged in absence. His heart swelled with a bittersweet blend of emotions as he engaged in conversation with Crystal, the eldest of the trio who was eighteen at the time. Basic inquiries flowed between them—questions of employment, upbringing and community—each word a tentative step towards understanding and acceptance.

Meanwhile, Delvan and Nia, who were aged fourteen and nine respectively, sat in quiet contemplation, their presence a silent testament to the depths of Derrick 's longing for familial connection. Despite the absence of shared memories, Derrick found solace in the sight of Nia, her innocence and sweetness a poignant reminder of the sisterly bond he had longed to cultivate.

Yet, amidst the fleeting moments of connection, Derrick found himself grappling with the harsh reality of their shared estrangement. The hope of forging meaningful relationships with his siblings was tempered by the sobering realization that time and distance had erected barriers that could not be easily traversed. The absence of shared experiences loomed large, casting a shadow over their tentative attempts at reconciliation.

As he reflected on their encounter, he realized that the road to a connection was bristled with obstacles—obstacles born of years spent apart and the scars of fractured relationships. The idealized vision of sibling camaraderie gave way to the stark reality of their fragmented bond, a bond shaped by the absence of shared memories and the weight of unspoken regrets.

Yet, amidst the challenges, he remained steadfast in his resolve to cultivate meaningful connections with his siblings, regardless of the obstacles that lay in their path. Though the road ahead would be filled with uncertainty, Derrick held onto the hope that with time and perseverance, their shared journey towards reconciliation would yield the fruits of love and understanding.

As the visit came to an end, he bid farewell to his siblings but carried with him seeds of hope—seeds planted in the fertile soil of their shared history, waiting to blossom into the vibrant tapestry of familial connection. He remained steadfast in his belief that, with love and patience, the bonds of sibling hood would transcend the barriers of time and distance, uniting them in the shared embrace of family once more.

8

A Distant Connection

As Derrick transitioned into his early twenties, the passage of time brought with it a familiar routine—a routine punctuated by sporadic encounters with his father, James, whose presence loomed large in their shared workspace. Despite the proximity that brought them face-to-face on a regular basis, he couldn't shake the gnawing sense of disconnect that lingered between them—a disconnect that manifested in the absence of any meaningful effort on James's part to foster a relationship.

Their interactions, confined to brief exchanges on the street that lacked the depth and intimacy that Derrick yearned for—a mere semblance of connection that left Derrick feeling adrift in a sea of unresolved longing. In these fleeting moments, conversation revolved around surface-level inquiries—superficial pleasantries that did little to bridge the chasm of separation that divided father and son.

Derrick 's hopes for reconciliation were buoyed by the possibility of a shared meal—a simple gesture that held the promise of forging bonds which transcended the boundaries of blood ties. Yet, as the years passed, his expectations were met with disappointment, as James failed to extend an invitation that would bring together his scattered brood of children residing in Dominica.

The absence of initiative on James's part left Derrick grappling with a sense of resignation—a resignation that mirrored the growing realization that the ties he longed for would remain elusive, drifting further from his grasp with each passing day. The hope of nurturing a relationship with his father and siblings dwindled, eclipsed by the shadows of apathy and neglect.

As he observed his father's continued adherence to a lifestyle marked by indifference and stagnation, a sense of disillusionment gnawed at his soul. Despite nearing the twilight years of his life, James showed no signs of change or growth—a stark reminder of the futility of Derrick 's efforts to bridge the chasm of estrangement.

The specter of disappointment loomed large in Derrick 's heart, casting a pall over his aspirations for reconciliation. With each passing year, the prospect of forging meaningful connections with his father and siblings seemed increasingly remote—a distant dream eclipsed by the harsh realities of their fractured bond.

His relationship with Crystal, Delvan, and Nia mirrored the tenuous nature of his connection with his father—a connection marred by the absence of shared experiences and the weight of unspoken grievances. Despite his best efforts to cultivate a sense of kinship, Derrick found himself grappling with a sense of disconnection—a disconnection that echoed the void left by James's neglect.

At times, his feelings towards his father bordered on disdain—a sentiment born of frustration and disappointment at James's refusal to acknowledge the opportunity for reconciliation. As James approached the milestone of seventy years, Derrick couldn't help but feel a pang of resentment towards the man who seemed content to let their relationship languish in a state of perpetual indifference.

Amidst the turmoil of unresolved emotions, Derrick found solace in the knowledge that, despite the absence of familial bonds, he was not defined by the shortcomings of his father. In the crucible of disappointment, he forged a path of resilience— a path illuminated by the guiding light of self-discovery and personal growth.

Though the glimmer of hope for reconciliation with his father remained faint, Derrick refused to succumb to despair. Instead, he embraced the journey of self-acceptance, recognizing that true family bonds transcended the limitations of blood ties, rooted instead in the fertile soil of love, forgiveness, and understanding.

As he navigated the complexities of estrangement, he emerged with a newfound sense of strength—a strength born of resilience in the face of adversity, and an unwavering belief in the transformative power of love. Though the road ahead remained filled with uncertainty, Derrick faced the future with courage and conviction, secure in the knowledge that, no matter the obstacles they faced, the bonds of family would endure, resilient and unwavering in the face of adversity.

9

Nuptial Crossroads

As Derrick reached the milestone of twenty-eight years, he found himself at a crossroads—a juncture where the promise of love and the complexities of ties converged in a delicate dance of decision-making. It was a time of transition, marked by the blossoming of romance with Lisa, a woman whose kindness and grace captivated his heart.

Their love was steeped in the shared foundation of faith, served as a symbol of brighter days ahead amidst the shadows of Derrick 's past—a past haunted by the specter of familial estrangement and the longing for connection. Together, Derrick and Lisa embarked on a journey of love and commitment, their hearts intertwined with shared dreams and aspirations.

With the decision to unite their lives in matrimony, Derrick and Lisa set a date for their wedding. This would be a day that marked the culmination of their love story and the beginning of a new chapter in their lives. Yet, amidst the joyous anticipation of their impending nuptials, he found himself battling with a dilemma, one that forced him to confront the ghosts of his past and the complexities of his familial relationships.

The question of whether to extend an invitation to his father loomed large in his mind. This decision was loaded with the weight of unresolved emotions and the uncertainty of reconciliation. Despite the tumultuous history that had characterized their relationship, he found the courage to extend an olive branch, inviting his father to bear witness to the union of the hearts of his and soon to be wife.

Yet, even as he extended this gesture of goodwill, he found himself wrestling with another dilemma—the question of whether to invite his siblings, Crystal, Delvan, and Nia. The prospect of their attendance at the wedding stirred a maelstrom of conflicting emotions within Derrick 's heart, as he wrestled with the fear that their presence would only serve to highlight the gaping chasm that divided them.

In the end, he made the difficult decision to invite only one sibling, Crystal, a choice born of a desire to honor the tenuous bond they had forged over the years, despite the awkwardness that threatened to overshadow their reunion. It was a decision tinged with regret, as he lamented the peculiar position in which his father's actions had placed him—a position loaded with the weight of unspoken grievances and unresolved longing.

As the wedding day drew near, he found himself navigating a maze of emotions—joy mingled with sorrow, hope tempered by regret. Yet, amidst the uncertainty, there remained a glimmer of hope, born of the belief that love had the power to transcend the barriers of distance and discord, uniting hearts in a shared celebration of love and commitment.

On the day of their wedding, Derrick stood at the threshold of a new beginning, his heart filled with a mixture of anticipation and trepidation. As he exchanged vows with Lisa, he found solace in the knowledge that, no matter the challenges they faced, their love would serve as a beacon of light, guiding them through the trials and tribulations of life's journey.

In the quiet moments of reflection that followed, Derrick found himself embracing a newfound sense of acceptance—a acceptance of the many complexities of parental relationships and the realization that despite the scars of the past, love had the power to heal and reconcile. He looked towards the future and vowed to nurture the bonds of love and connection that bound them together, forging a path of unity and understanding that would go beyond the confines of blood ties and lineal expectations.

10

A Father's Betrayal

As the sun cast its golden glow upon the day wedding day, anticipation hung heavy in the air, mingling with the scent of blossoming flowers and the murmur of whispered vows. Yet, amidst the joyous celebration of love and unity, a dark cloud loomed on the horizon—a cloud borne of the unsettling presence of his father, James, whose attendance at the wedding would soon prove to be a source of profound disappointment and anguish.

Reluctantly, Derrick extended an invitation to his father, offering him a platform to share in the joyous festivities of their union. Yet, as James took to the stage to deliver his speech, Derrick 's hopes were swiftly dashed by the venomous words that spilled from his father's lips—a speech that would go down in infamy as one of the worst displays of paternal neglect and self-centeredness.

With each word uttered, James made it abundantly clear that his presence at the wedding was little more than a self-indulgent exercise in narcissism. Rather than offering words of wisdom or heartfelt blessings, James seized the spotlight to regale the attendees with tales of his bachelorhood, callously boasting of his freedom and independence.

The speech, devoid of any semblance of parental pride or affection, served only to further underscore the depths of James's indifference towards his son's happiness. Instead of celebrating his union with Lisa, James callously dredged up the sordid details of Derrick 's conception—a cruel reminder of the scars of the past that Derrick had long sought to bury.

As anger boiled within Derrick 's veins, he found himself on the brink of explosive confrontation, his indignation reaching a crescendo as James stubbornly clung to the microphone, despite Derrick 's desperate pleas for him to relinquish it. The scene unfolded in a tableau of humiliation and shame, casting a pall over the festivities and staining the sanctity of Derrick 's wedding day.

The repercussions of James's actions reverberated throughout the reception, casting a shadow over the joyous celebration of love and unity. As Derrick and Lisa sat at the head table, their hearts heavy with the weight of disappointment, James approached with a disarming smile—a smile that belied the callous disregard he had shown for his son's happiness.

With audacity that bordered on insolence, James reached out to Derrick, his outstretched hand poised to pilfer a morsel from his son's plate—an act of brazen entitlement that left Derrick seething with silent fury. Though he clenched the fork tightly in his hand, Derrick remained composed, his voice calm as he rebuffed his father's presumptuous request.

"I won't eat it all," James murmured, Derrick was laden with unspoken resentment and frustration. In that moment, as thoughts of retaliation flickered in the recesses of his mind, Derrick resolved to rise above his father's provocation, determined not to allow his toxic presence to tarnish the sanctity of his wedding day.

Yet, despite Derrick 's outward composure, the wounds inflicted by his father's callous disregard ran deep, leaving an indelible mark on the fabric of their relationship. In the aftermath of the wedding, Derrick grappled with a sense of profound regret—a regret born of the realization that, in extending an olive branch to his father, he had only invited further pain and disappointment into his life.

As Derrick sifted through the digital images of his wedding day, he made the painful decision to crop his father out of some of the photographs—a symbolic gesture of defiance against the man who had betrayed his trust and shattered his dreams. Though the scars of his father's actions would linger, Derrick remained steadfast in his commitment to building a future filled with love, forgiveness, and the unwavering resolve to rise above the shadows of the past.

11

A Struggle with a Father's Indifference

As the sands of time continued to trickle through the hourglass of Derrick 's life, the tenuous thread that bound him to his father remained unchanged—a static tableau of unfulfilled hopes and dashed expectations. Despite his earnest efforts to bridge the chasm of estrangement, his relationship with his father stagnated, mired in the quagmire of indifference and neglect.

There was an unforeseen encounter between Derrick 's wife, Lisa, and his father, James, in the midst of their daily routines. Lisa, working as a secretary at the police commissioner's office where James was employed as a police officer, inadvertently became caught up in the complex web of tension that had haunted Derrick for years.

In a twist of fate, Lisa's daily encounters with James served as a sobering reminder of the fragile threads that bound Derrick to his father—a reminder that, despite their shared bloodlines, the bond between father and son remained frayed and brittle, teetering on the precipice of irrelevance.

The initial exchange between Lisa and James unfolded in a tableau of polite indifference—a fleeting moment of recognition marred by the spectre of unspoken grievances. As Lisa extended a courteous greeting to James, his response was tinged with a hint of surprise, his calm demeanour masking the underlying tension that simmered beneath the surface.

"Oh, my goodness, darling, I did not realize it was you," James's words rang out in the stillness of the workspace, a hollow echo of paternal recognition that fell short of the mark. Yet, despite the fleeting moment of connection, the gulf between them remained impassable—a silent testament to the chasm of estrangement that divided father and son.

In the ensuing days, Derrick found himself unwittingly drawn into the orbit of his father's presence, as the routine of dropping Lisa off at work each morning brought him face-to-face with the man whose indifference had left an indelible mark on his soul. With each passing interaction, Derrick 's hopes for reconciliation dwindled, replaced by a resigned acceptance of the status quo—a status quo defined by the absence of meaningful connection and the weight of unspoken regret.

Despite his best efforts to bridge the gap, Derrick found himself stymied by his father's reticence, that mirrored the depths of their fractured relationship. Attempts at conversation were met with terse responses, each word a barrier that served only to deepen the chasm between them.

As he stood before his father's security booth, grappling with the silence that enveloped them like a suffocating shroud, he couldn't help but feel a pang of disappointment which was born of the realization that despite their shared proximity, the distance between them remained in surmount.

12

Long-Awaited Blessing

Three years had passed since Derrick and Lisa exchanged vows, their union blossoming with the promise of love and companionship. Yet, amidst the ebb and flow of their shared journey, a new chapter was set to unfold—a chapter imbued with the tender whispers of anticipation and the palpable joy of impending parenthood.

The news of Lisa's pregnancy sent ripples of elation coursing through Derrick 's soul—a tidal wave of emotion that threatened to overwhelm him with its sheer magnitude. For Derrick, the prospect of fatherhood was more than just a dream fulfilled—it was a lifelong yearning, a whispered prayer uttered in the quiet recesses of his heart.

As Lisa tenderly delivered the news of their impending arrival, tears of joy cascaded down Derrick 's cheeks, each droplet a testament to the depth of his longing and the overwhelming gratitude that filled his soul. It was a moment of profound emotion, one he had yearned for years, when the mere thought of fatherhood brought tears to his eyes.

The day Aiden entered the world was a symphony of emotions—a crescendo of joy and wonder that echoed through the hallowed halls of the hospital. As Derrick cradled his newborn son in his arms, the weight of responsibility and love intertwined in a delicate dance, binding father and son in an unbreakable bond.

With each gentle caress and whispered promise, Derrick vowed to be a steadfast presence in Aiden's life—a beacon of love and guidance, steering him through the trials and triumphs of childhood and beyond. For Derrick, fatherhood was not merely a role to be fulfilled, but a sacred duty and a commitment to cherish and protect his son with every fiber of his being.

Amidst the whirlwind of diaper changes and sleepless nights, Derrick found solace in the quiet moments shared with his son—a tender reminder of the precious gift bestowed upon him by the hands of fate. As Aiden grew from a newborn infant into a spirited three-year-old, Derrick marveled at the boundless wonder and curiosity that lit up his son's eyes, each moment a precious treasure to be cherished for a lifetime.

Yet, amidst the joy of parenthood, Derrick found himself still struggling with the complexities of his relationship with his own father—a relationship fraught with unspoken grievances and unresolved emotions. Though he continued to drop Lisa off at work each morning, the specter of his father's presence loomed large, casting a shadow over their shared routine.

In a silent gesture of reconciliation, Derrick would often roll down the windows of their car as they passed by his father's post, hoping to bridge the gap between generations with a simple exchange of greetings. Yet, despite his best efforts, Derrick found himself unable to summon the courage to introduce his son to his grandfather—a testament to the lingering wounds of the past that had yet to heal.

As Derrick navigated the complexities of parenthood, he found himself grappling with a sense of ambivalence—a delicate balancing act between the joys of newfound fatherhood and the lingering shadows of his own upbringing. Yet, in the midst the turmoil, he remained steadfast in his resolve to break the cycle of discord, forging a path of love and acceptance for his son to follow.

In the quiet moments of reflection that followed, Derrick found solace in the knowledge that, despite the scars of the past, he possessed the power to shape his son's future—to instil in him the values of compassion, forgiveness, and unconditional love that had eluded him in his own upbringing.

As Derrick gazed into the innocent eyes of his son, he vowed to be the father he had always longed for—a beacon of strength and compassion, guiding Aiden through the trials and tribulations of life with unwavering love and devotion. Though the road ahead remained filled with uncertainty, Derrick faced the future with courage and determination, secure in the knowledge that, no matter the obstacles they faced, the bond between father and son would endure, resilient and unbreakable in the face of adversity.

13

Secret Struggle

Five years had passed since Derrick 's marriage to Lisa, a union marked by the gentle ebb and flow of shared dreams and whispered promises. Yet, amidst the tranquil rhythm of their lives, a shadow loomed on the horizon—a shadow cast by the specter of illness that threatened to shatter the fragile veneer of normalcy.

As Derrick and Lisa continued their daily routines, the familiar presence of Derrick 's father, James, lingered in the corridors of their shared existence. Unbeknownst to them, James had been secretly battling with a silent adversary—a blood clot in his leg that kept him sidelined from work, his absence a harbinger of the storm that lay ahead.

Initially, Derrick and Lisa had assumed that James's frequent absences were merely the result of his demanding work schedule— a misconception that would soon be shattered by the harsh reality of illness. It was only when Derrick mustered the courage to reach out to his father that the truth began to emerge—a truth veiled in the solemn words of a son reaching out to his father in a time of need.

As James shared updates from his doctor, Derrick listened with a heavy heart, his concern mingling with a sense of helplessness as he tussled with the gravity of his father's condition. Yet, even as James assured Derrick of his imminent return to work, the shadow of uncertainty loomed large, casting a cloud over their shared conversation.

Unknown to most, James harboured a secret that weighed heavily on his soul, threatening to consume him from within. For nestled within the recesses of his body lurked a silent foe—a diagnosis of prostate cancer that had remained hidden from the prying eyes of family and friends.

As the cancer stealthily crept through his body, James found himself fighting with a sense of isolation—a solitary struggle waged in the shadows, far removed from the prying eyes of those he held dear. Though his friends and family grew concerned by his apparent illness, they remained unaware of the silent battle that raged within him, a battle fought with quiet dignity and unwavering resolve.

In the quiet moments of reflection that followed, Derrick found himself wrestling with a torrent of conflicting emotions—anger, sadness, and a profound sense of betrayal. How could his father keep such a devastating diagnosis hidden from those who loved him most? The revelation shook Derrick to his core, shattering the illusion of normalcy that had cloaked their shared existence.

Yet, amidst the turmoil, Derrick found solace in the knowledge that, despite the darkness that threatened to engulf them, he possessed the strength and resilience to weather the storm. With each passing day, he resolved to stand by his father's side, offering unwavering support and unconditional love in the face of adversity.

As James's illness progressed to an advanced stage, Derrick found himself drawn into the fray, his heart heavy with the weight of impending loss. Yet, amidst the pain and uncertainty, there remained a glimmer of hope—a hope born of the enduring strength of familial love and the unwavering bond between father and son.

In the crucible of adversity, Derrick found himself confronted with a profound revelation—a revelation that transcended the boundaries of family discord and ushered in a new era of understanding and reconciliation. Despite the tumultuous nature of his relationship with his father, Derrick 's unwavering commitment to his Christian values compelled him to honour his father, flaws and all, in a gesture of compassion and forgiveness.

As James's illness cast a long shadow over their shared existence, Derrick embarked on a journey of healing and redemption—a journey that would lead him to the doorstep of his father's solitary abode, where the echoes of unspoken grievances gave way to the gentle whispers of shared stories and cherished memories.

With each visit, a barrier was broken—a barrier forged by years of silence and misunderstanding as he and his father engaged in heartfelt conversations that laid bare the raw emotions and untold truths that had long simmered beneath the surface. In the quiet moments of their shared companionship, Derrick found himself drawn into the mesh of his father's life, weaving together the threads of past regrets and forgotten dreams with the gentle touch of empathy and understanding.

James opened up about his own childhood and the trials he had faced and Derrick listened with an attentive ear and open heart, his own struggles mirrored in the unspoken yearnings of his father's soul. Through tales of his love for cricket and his days as a schoolteacher, James revealed the hidden depths of his character—a character shaped by the scars of a fractured relationship with his own father, a relationship marked by absence and longing.

In the crucible of their shared vulnerability, Derrick and his father found solace in the unspoken bond that united them—a bond forged by the shared burdens of regret and the enduring hope of redemption. As James reflected on his own life, Derrick bore witness to the raw emotions that lay bare in his father's words—a testament to the profound impact of unresolved pain and unspoken truths.

Yet, amidst the weight of regret and the burden of unfulfilled dreams, Derrick remained steadfast in his commitment to his father's well-being, offering comfort and companionship in the face of uncertainty. From running errands to sharing heartfelt prayers, Derrick stood by his father's side, offering a beacon of light in the darkness of illness and despair.

As the days turned into weeks and the cancer continued its

relentless march through James's body, Derrick found himself drawn into the embrace of his father's family—a family he had long yearned to know. In the warmth of their shared companionship, Derrick discovered a sense of belonging—a sense of connection that transcended the confines of bloodlines and familial ties.

With each encounter, Derrick 's heart expanded with newfound love and understanding, as he bore witness to the enduring strength of familial bonds forged in the crucible of adversity. Through the loving care of his father's sister Frances and the gentle embrace of his newfound aunts, James found solace in the knowledge that he was not alone—a knowledge that brought him comfort in the darkest hours of his illness.

In the quiet moments of reflection that followed, Derrick found himself humbled by the transformative power of forgiveness and redemption—a power that had breathed new life into the fractured bonds of father and son. As James's journey drew to a close, Derrick stood by his father's side, a pillar of strength and unwavering support, his heart filled with gratitude for the opportunity to walk this path of healing and reconciliation.

And though the road ahead remained fraught with uncertainty, Derrick faced the future with courage and determination, secure in the knowledge that no matter the obstacles they faced, the enduring strength of their bond would carry them through the darkest of nights and into the light of a new dawn.

14

A Son's Grace and A Father's Redemption

As James's health continued to decline, Derrick found himself drawn deeper into the tumultuous currents of his father's suffering—a journey full of pain and uncertainty yet buoyed by the enduring bond of love and compassion that bound father and son together.

With each passing day, James's condition grew increasingly dire, until he could no longer tend to his own needs and sought refuge in the loving care of his sister Mary—a beacon of solace in the storm of his suffering. Bedridden and wracked with excruciating pain, James's cries echoed through the halls of his sister's home, a haunting reminder of the relentless march of illness and despair.

For Derrick, these were harrowing times—times marked by the stark reality of his father's suffering and the profound weight of his own helplessness in the face of this misfortune. Yet, amidst the darkness, a flicker of hope remained—a hope born of the unbreakable bond that united father and son in their shared journey of redemption.

As Derrick observed his father's suffering, he felt compelled to become involved in the tender duties of caregiving—providing relief and reassurance through gentle gestures and whispered prayers, pleading for divine intervention. During brief respites, Derrick would sit beside his father's bed, his own heart burdened by unspoken sorrow and indescribable anguish. In the quiet moments, he listened as his father softly repeated the words, "Have mercy on me lord, Have mercy on me." Those words brought him comfort, knowing that his father sought repentance.

It was during one such visit that Derrick found himself joined by Crystal and Lisa, their presence a testament to the enduring strength of family while dealing with this affliction. As Lisa tenderly inquired about his father's deepest desires, Derrick 's heart swelled with emotion—a torrent of longing and regret unleashed in the quiet confines of his father's room.

Through tear-stained eyes, James poured out his heart to his loved ones, his voice trembling with the weight of unspoken regrets and untold dreams. In a moment of raw vulnerability, he cried out to God for mercy, his words a plea for forgiveness and redemption in the twilight of his suffering.

For Derrick, the moment was a crucible of emotion—a poignant reminder of the fragility of life and the enduring power of love to transcend even the darkest of nights. As he stood by his father's side, Derrick found ease in the knowledge that, despite the pain and suffering that lay ahead, his father had been granted the precious gift of time—to heal emotionally, to repent, to reconcile and to find peace in the embrace of his Creator.

As the weeks slipped by and James's condition continued to deteriorate, Derrick remained a steadfast presence by his father's side remaining that beacon of hope in the gathering storm of illness and despair. Through whispered prayers and gentle reassurances, he sought to ease his father's suffering, offering comfort and solace in the face of unimaginable pain.

And though the cancer had taken a toll on James's body, leaving him unrecognizable to those who knew him best, Derrick remained steadfast in his commitment to his father's well-being, a testament to the enduring strength of love and the redemptive power of grace in the face of adversity.

As the first rays of dawn gently filtered through the curtains of Derrick 's bedroom, he awoke to a message that would forever alter the course of his journey—a message that bore the weight of sorrow and the promise of eternal peace. It was June 7th, 2021, a day etched in the annals of Derrick 's memory as the day his father, James, breathed his last breath, succumbing to the relentless onslaught of cancer in the early hours of the morning.

For Derrick, the news came as a bittersweet revelation—a testament to the fragile nature of life and the inevitability of mortality. Yet, amidst the waves of grief that threatened to overwhelm him, Derrick found consolation in the belief that his father had risen above the confines of earthly suffering, finding eternal rest in the embrace of his Creator.

Though tears flowed freely down Derrick 's cheeks, mingling with the echoes of unspoken prayers and whispered blessings, he took comfort in the knowledge that his father was no longer shackled by the chains of pain and suffering. In the quiet moments of reflection that followed, Derrick found himself drawn into the gentle embrace of faith—a faith that whispered of a love that goes beyond even the darkest of nights.

As Derrick grappled with the enormity of his loss, he found himself enveloped in a sense of peace—a peace born of the knowledge that his father's journey had not ended with death but had merely begun anew in the boundless expanse of eternity. Though the void left by his father's passing would never be filled, Derrick took solace in the belief that his father's spirit would live on in the hearts and minds of those who loved him most.

15

Farewell to Sweet Papa

As the sombre chords of grief echoed through the familiar spaces that James had occupied, Derrick found himself immersed in the solemn task of planning his father's final farewell—a journey marked by the delicate dance of remembrance and reflection, of sorrow and celebration.

Together with his sister Crystal and their aunt Mary, he took the helm in orchestrating the funeral arrangements—a labour of love and devotion that bore witness to the enduring bond that united them in their shared grief. Through tear-stained eyes and whispered prayers, they navigated the intricate details of James's final journey, drawing strength from the memories they held dear and the love that bound them together.

As they gathered to bid their final farewell to James, Derrick found himself enveloped in a sense of reverence and solemnity— a reverence born of the knowledge that his father's life had touched so many hearts and souls, leaving behind a legacy of love and laughter that would endure long after his passing.

With the precision of a well-choreographed symphony, the

funeral procession unfolded—a solemn march of police officers and family members making their way to the hallowed sanctuary of the church. Against the backdrop of grief and loss, they paid homage to a man who had served his community with honour and distinction as a teacher for twenty-six years—a man whose life had been a testament to the values of courage and compassion, of duty and devotion. A man with a passion for reading who maintained strict standards in grammar with his students earned the nickname of his favourite and renowned author, Gore Vidal and the title Teacher James.

As they entered the sanctuary, Derrick's gaze fell upon the faces of his siblings—his brothers and sisters, united in their grief yet bound by the unbreakable ties of blood and kinship. Though some were absent, their presence was felt in the quiet whispers of love and remembrance that echoed through the sacred space.

The theme of the funeral, the colour green was fastened on all who attended—a tribute to James's favourite colour, a symbol of life and renewal that spoke to the essence of his spirit. Against the backdrop of verdant hues, Derrick found comfort in the knowledge that his father's legacy would live on in the hearts and minds of those who had been touched by his presence.

As the tributes and eulogy were being shared, Derrick sat in reverent silence, his heart heavy with the weight of unspoken emotion. With each word uttered, he found echoes of his father's life reflected in his own life—a life marked by discipline and dedication, by laughter and tears.

With tears in his eyes, he absorbed the eulogy delivered by his father's niece, portraying a man who had embraced life with fervour and determination—a man whose kindness and empathy had left a lasting impact on countless lives. Reflecting on his father's roles as both educator and law enforcement officer, Derrick couldn't help but lament his father's reluctance to extend the same dedication to his own children. Amid the solemn atmosphere of the church, Derrick felt himself becoming entwined in the intricate fabric of his father's legacy, memories and yearning with tender affection and reminiscence.

As the eulogy drew to a close, Derrick 's emotions threatened to overwhelm him—a tide of grief and longing that surged within him, threatening to consume him whole. Yet, even as tears welled in his eyes, he remained steadfast in his resolve, a testament to the strength of his spirit and the depth of his love.

And as he sat in the quiet sanctuary of the church, Derrick whispered a silent prayer of farewell—a prayer that spoke of love and gratitude, of sorrow and peace. For in that sacred space, surrounded by the echoes of grief and loss, he found peace in the knowledge that his father's journey had not ended with death, but had merely begun anew in the boundless expanse of eternity.

In the days that followed, Derrick found himself navigating the delicate dance of grief and acceptance—a journey marked by the gentle rhythms of mourning and remembrance. As he stood by his father's graveside, surrounded by the solemn silence of the cemetery, he offered a silent prayer for the soul of his beloved father—a prayer that spoke of love and forgiveness, of hope and redemption.

Though the pain of loss lingered like a shadow in the recesses of Derrick 's heart, he found strength in the brief memories he shared with his father—a knit of moments woven together by the threads of love and laughter, of joy and sorrow. With each passing day, he sought to honour his father's legacy, carrying forth the lessons he had imparted with unwavering determination and boundless gratitude.

As he reflected on his father's life, he found himself drawn to the quiet moments he spent with him during his illness and the enduring grace of a Creator who connected them both in James's final days.

Though the ache of loss remained a constant companion in Derrick 's heart, he found comfort in the belief that his father's spirit would continue to guide him along the winding paths of life—a beacon of light in the darkness, illuminating the way forward with the gentle glow of love and remembrance. And though the road ahead remained uncertain, he faced the future with courage and determination, secure in the knowledge that, no matter the challenges that lay ahead, his father's spirit would walk beside him, a silent guardian, and a cherished companion on the journey of life.

16

Echoes of Love and Loss

In the gentle embrace of time's passage, we find ourselves standing at the threshold of eternity, where pain and suffering dissolve into the ether, and memories linger like whispers in the wind. It has been over two years since James's bid farewell to this mortal coil, departing for the heavenly banquet to reunite with his Maker. In that sacred realm beyond, where time knows no bounds, we hold onto the hope that one day, his children, family, and friends will once again behold his gentle smile and loving embrace.

In the quiet moments of reflection, my heart echoes with the melody of longing—a symphony of love and loss, woven into the fabric of eternity. And though the road ahead may be filled with shadows, I find comfort in the knowledge that love endures, rising above the boundaries of time and space, uniting hearts in a sacred dance of remembrance and hope.

When the skies are clear and the clouds open to heaven's doors, I look up and quietly whisper, "Daddy, I believe I will see you again someday, I am longing for your love."

Lisa had revealed your confession to which was made to a colleague, one whom you were very close to and loved as your own – one of your deepest regrets is not being there for me. Aunty Mary also revealed that you cried out my name in your final days.

I longed for your presence as a child, aching for the guidance and affection that were but a distant dream. Your absence left a pain etched deep within, a void that no earthly comfort could fill. Yet, amidst the hurt and longing, there is still a glimmer of hope that one day, our souls would intertwine once more in the sweet embrace of eternity.

I longed for you, Daddy, I missed you, I yearned for your love and guidance. But something kept us apart, a barrier we could not breach. Now, in the quiet of your absence, I realize how much I long for you, how deeply I love you. It hurts knowing that you are not here to proofread by book Teacher James.

With tainted dreams lying within the conscious and subconscious, tattooed words on every fibre of my being and a still heart one thing remains:

Breaking the chains of generational curses is a poignant journey, one that often requires us to confront our deepest fears and vulnerabilities. For me, this journey took on a new meaning in the wake of my father's passing, as I grappled with the realization that our strained relationship was a casualty of his own unspoken pain and unresolved wounds.

In the quiet moments of reflection, I found myself haunted by the specter of missed opportunities, the echoes of words left unspoken, and gestures left unmade weighing heavily on my heart. It was a harsh awakening, a stark reminder of the fragility of time and the preciousness of the bonds that bind us together.

As I sifted through the fragments of memories and emotions, I came to a profound realization: I had waited far too long for my father to make the first move, to extend the olive branch of reconciliation. But now, in the aftermath of his departure from this world, I understood that he too carried the burden of unfulfilled longing, the silent yearning for connection that remained unvoiced.

In a moment of startling clarity, my father's words echoed in my mind, a poignant confession of his own fractured relationship with his father, a man he barely knew. The weight of that revelation settled upon me like a heavy cloak, the realization dawning that the cycle of estrangement and absence had been perpetuated across generations, a silent legacy of pain and isolation.

But amidst the shadows of the past, there flickered a glimmer of hope, a beacon of light illuminating the path forward. For in the faces of my wife, my son, my mother, and my siblings, I saw the opportunity for redemption, the chance to break free from the shackles of the past and forge a new legacy of love and connection.

With tears in my eyes and a trembling heart, I reached out to my siblings and mother, extending a hand of reconciliation and forgiveness, determined to bridge the divide that had long separated us. And as they enveloped me in their embrace, I felt the weight of decades of separation and misunderstanding melt away, replaced by a profound sense of belonging and acceptance.

In that moment, I vowed to cherish every precious moment, to nurture the bonds of love and family that had been so nearly lost. For I knew now, with a certainty born of hard-won wisdom, that the greatest legacy we can leave behind is not one of pain and regret, but of love and connection, spanning across generations like a beacon of hope in the darkness.

Aiden my son you are a pillar of encouragement amidst the shadows of grief. With each passing day, your laughter fills the void left by your grandfather's absence, a reminder of the generations bound by love's enduring thread. I dream of a future where your path is paved with love and light, a legacy of hope to break the chains of generations past.

And to my siblings, scattered like stars across the sky, my heart reaches out in silent longing:

"Rose, Yasmin, Manuel, Gisellc, Sheldon, Emma, Crystal, Delvan, Ethan, Nia—I long for you all. Each of you holds a piece of my heart, a memory woven into the fabric of my being. Though miles may separate us, know that my love for you endures, a flame that burns bright in the darkness."

"Mummy, I longed for you, yearned for your presence. Now, as I hold you close to me, I am reminded of the strength and grace that you imparted to me. Thank you for the gift of life, for the love that knows no bounds."

"My dear Lisa, my precious Lilly, my love for you surpasses

mere words. Within your arms, I discover solace and resilience, a guiding light through life's darkest moments. I am grateful for the gift of your love, for your unwavering presence beside me, offering comfort during my father's absence. Thank you."

"Thank you, Blessed Mother, for guiding me with your love. In your gentle embrace, I find comfort and peace, a refuge from the storms of life. I love you, now and always."

"Jesus, I long for you, more than words can express. In your presence, I find my strength, my hope, my joy. Thank you for being the father I needed when my earthly one was not present. As I meditate on your love, I am reminded of the psalmist's words: 'As a deer pants for the water, so my soul longs after you.' You alone are my one desire, my heart's truest longing."

17

Epilogue

Longing Hearts: A Poetic Journey of Love and Loss

In the hushed whispers of memory's embrace,
   I find myself lost in the echoes of your grace.
   It's been over two years since you bid farewell,
   Yet your presence lingers, a bittersweet tale to tell.

Oh Daddy, how I longed for you,
   Yearning for a love I never knew.
   As a child, I craved your guiding hand,
   But you were absent, like grains of sand.

Lisa, my sweet Lilly, how you were told,
   Of your colleague's words, a story untold.
   Your heart swelled with joy at our conversation rare,
   Yet I never knew, until you were no longer there.

Aunty Mary whispered of your final plea,

Crying out my name, in agony.
Oh Daddy, how I wish I had known,
That you desired a bond, not left alone.

My son Aiden, a reflection of you,
With his love for books, pure and true.
I've taken up writing, a newfound art,
But, Oh how I wish you were here to impart.

Rose, Yasmin, Manuel, and more,
Siblings dear, my heart's core.
I long for the love you could have shared,
In the moments we missed, and the bonds we spared.

Mummy, I long for your embrace,
For the love that time cannot erase.
Thank you for bringing me into this world,
Forever honoured, your love unfurled.

Aiden, my son, my hope, my light,
I long for your future, shining bright.
To break the chains of the past, I vow,
For you, my child, I take this solemn vow.

Lisa, my sweet Lilly, my guiding star,
In your love, I find solace afar.
I long for your touch, your gentle grace,
In the warmth of your love, I find my place.

Blessed mother, guide me through,
With your love, forever true.

In your arms, I find my rest,
Forever cherished, forever blessed.

And Jesus, my Savior, my King,
In your love, my soul takes wing.
I long for you, with every breath,
In your presence, I find my depth.

As a deer pants for the water's embrace,
So, my soul longs for your grace.
In you, I find my eternal fire.
You alone are my heart's desire,

In the echoes of longing hearts,
I find solace in love's sacred arts.
Though parted by time's gentle hand,
In love's embrace, we'll forever stand.